How We Got the Bible

Participant Guide

Timothy Paul Jones, PhD

Developed by Garrick Bailey

This Participant Guide accompanies the
How We Got the Bible 6-Session DVD-Based Study
(ISBN 9781628622072 or 9781628622065)

How We Got the Bible Participant Guide
Copyright ©2015 Bristol Works, Inc.
Rose Publishing, LLC
P.O. Box 3473
Peabody, Massachusetts 01961-3473 USA
www.hendricksonrose.com

This book is published in association with Nappaland Literary Agency, an independent agency dedicated to publishing works that are: Authentic. Relevant. Eternal. Visit us on the web at Nappaland.com.

Unless otherwise indicated, Scripture quotations are taken from *The Holy Bible, English Standard Version.* Copyright ©2000; 2001 by Crossway Bibles, a division of Good News Publishers. Used by permission. All rights reserved.

Printed in the United States of America

Contents

About This Study

Have you ever had a coworker ask you about books that were supposedly cut out of the Bible? Or maybe somebody tried to tell you that the person who *really* chose the books of the Bible was the Emperor Constantine. Maybe you've heard words like "inerrant" and "infallible" and you wonder what exactly do we mean when we say that the Bible is inerrant and infallible.

In this six-session study on *How We Got the Bible* you'll learn about all these things, plus a lot more. You'll learn how the books in your Bible ended up there, and why we can trust the text of the Old and New Testaments. You'll learn how the Bible was copied and translated, and the fascinating stories of people in history who risked their lives to spread the Word of God.

About the Author

Timothy Paul Jones , PhD, serves as the C. Edwin Gheens Professor of Christian Ministry and as associate vice president at The Southern Baptist Theological Seminary, the flagship school of the Southern Baptist Convention and one of the largest seminaries in the world. Before coming to Southern Seminary, Dr. Jones led churches in Missouri and Oklahoma as a pastor and an associate pastor.

Dr. Jones has authored or coauthored more than a dozen books in the fields of family ministry and apologetics, including the CBA bestseller *The Da Vinci Codebreaker.* In 2007, Charles Colson listed him as one of "four names you need to know" when responding to the new atheists. Christian Retailing Magazine awarded Jones top honors in 2010 in the Christian education category for his book *Christian History Made Easy.* Jones has also received the Scholastic Recognition Award from the North American Professors of Christian Education for his research in faith development.

The son of a rural pastor, Dr. Jones earned his bachelor of arts degree in biblical studies at Manhattan Christian College. He also holds the Master of Divinity degree from Midwestern Baptist Theological Seminary and the Doctor of Philosophy degree from The Southern Baptist Theological Seminary. He has taught biblical languages at Midwestern Baptist Theological Seminary and at Oklahoma Baptist University, as well as lecturing on the reliability of the New Testament Gospels at the University of North Carolina (Chapel Hill) at forums sponsored by InterVarsity Christian Fellowship.

Despite his academic background, Dr. Jones has shown a capacity to communicate to ordinary people in an appealing and accessible style. He has been interviewed on numerous radio and television programs, including WGN Morning News, Fox & Friends, Crosstalk America, and Bible Answer Man. Dr. Jones is married to Rayann and they have three daughters.

Garrick Bailey (ThM, Dallas Theological Seminary) is a PhD student in Systematic Theology at The Southern Baptist Theological Seminary. His research interests include the theology of the early church and Roman Catholicism. He serves on the editorial staff for the Center for Ancient Christian Studies and the *Journal of Discipleship and Family Ministry.* When he's not reading or drinking coffee—usually at the same time—you will find him spending time with his wife and two children.

5

About the Complete Kit

How We Got the Bible Complete Kit (ISBN 9781628622072) contains everything you need to get started:

- DVD with six 30-minute video sessions.

- Leader Guide (printed copy plus a PDF for your iPad or tablet)

- Participant Guide (printed) with session outlines, discussion and study questions, and extra information. Buy additional participant guides for each class member (ISBN 9781628622126).

- Reference handbook, *How We Got the Bible* (ISBN 9781628622164)

- Fold-out time line of the history of the Bible

- Ready-to-use PowerPoint® presentation with 100+ slides to expand the scope of teaching

- CD-ROM with printable PDFs of promotional posters, banners, fliers, handouts, and bulletin inserts.

Available at www.hendricksonrose.com or by calling Rose Publishing at 1-800-358-3111. Also available wherever good Christian books are sold.

SESSION 1

What's So Special about the Bible?

Get This: When Scripture speaks, God speaks.

"All Scripture is breathed out by God and profitable for teaching, for reproof, for correction, and for training in righteousness, that the man of God may be complete, equipped for every good work."—2 Timothy 3:16–17

Session 1 Outline

Use this session outline to follow along with the video and take notes.

1. The Bible is inspired.

   a. All Scripture is God-breathed (2 Timothy 3:14–16).

   b. Paul identifies a text that would become part of Luke's Gospel as Scripture (1 Timothy 5:18 and Luke 10:7).

   c. Peter identifies Paul's writings as Scripture (2 Peter 3:16).

   d. The authors wrote the words God intended, but in their own literary style.

2. The Bible is infallible and inerrant.

   a. Infallibility—"The Bible is unable to deceive" (John 10:35).

   b. Inerrancy—The Bible never errs.

3. The Bible is sufficient.

    a. Scripture *provides* what we need to know God.

    b. Scripture has been sufficiently *preserved*.

4. Scripture must transform us.

    a. Scripture is like a mirror (James 1:22–24).

    b. The Bible is dependent on *interpretation* and *illumination* for application (1 Peter 1:11).

Key Terms

Autographs—The original manuscripts of the Bible (from the Greek *autographos*, "written in one's own hand").

Illumination—The enlightening work of the Holy Spirit in the Christian person and community, enabling believers to understand and to obey the Scriptures.

Inerrancy—The Bible is completely trustworthy and contains no errors in the original autographs.

Infallibility—The Bible is incapable of deceiving us and will never fail in its purpose of revealing God and the way of salvation to humans.

Inspiration—The work of the Holy Spirit enabling the human authors of the Bible to record what God desired to have written in the Scriptures.

Interpretation—Explanation of the intended meaning of a text. The study of interpretation is known as "hermeneutics," from the Greek *hermeneuo* ("I translate").

Manuscript—A text copied by hand rather than printed using a printer or printing press.

Sufficiency—Scripture is sufficient in two senses: First and foremost, Scripture provides enough knowledge for us to find God's truth and to live in fellowship with him. Second, Scripture has been copied with enough accuracy to preserve God's truth.

Group Discussion

1. Why are the three truths regarding the Bible—inspiration, infallibility, and sufficiency—important? (Hint: Imagine if a believer or a church were to reject those three truths about the Bible. What kind of impact would that have on their Bible study, prayer habits, and daily life?)

2. Scripture can act like a mirror, showing us the truth about ourselves and spurring us to be doers of the Word not just hearers (James 1:22–24). Describe a time when God's Word worked like a mirror in your life.

3. The apostle Paul tells Timothy to "preach the word; be ready in season and out of season; reprove, rebuke, exhort, with great patience and instruction" (2 Timothy 4:2). What might this pattern look like in your life?

How We Got the Bible Quiz

Take this quiz before the session. You'll take this quiz again after the last class session. The purpose of this quiz is not to see how much you know now, but how much you've learned after completing all six sessions when you take the quiz again. (Answers will be given in the last session.)

1. How many books are in the Bible?

   _____ *66* _____

2. How many human authors wrote the books of the Bible?

   a. Fewer than 10
   b. Between 10 and 25
   c. At least 40
   d. More than 100

3. What do we call the original manuscripts of the Bible?

   _____ *Autographs* _____

4. How many original manuscripts of the Bible survive today?

   _____ *0* _____

5. In what language(s) was the Old Testament originally written?

   _____ *Aramaic & Hebrew* _____

6. In what language was the New Testament originally written?

   _____ *Greek & Hebrew* _____

7. What do we call the ancient Greek translation of the Old Testament?

LXX Septuagint

8. When did mass printing of Bibles begin?

   a. Before AD 300
   b. Around AD 650
   c. *After AD 1400*
   d. After AD 1750

9. How many ancient Greek manuscripts of the New Testament exist?

   a. Fewer than 1,000
   b. Between 1,000 and 2,500
   c. Between 2,500 and 5,000
   d. *More than 5,000*

10. Who is known as the "father of the English Bible"?

Tyndale, Wycliffe

Hear God's Word

2 Timothy 3:14–4:5

Study Notes

- The word translated "breathed out by God" (some translations read "inspired by God") combines the Greek words for "God" (*theos*) and "breathed" (*pneo*). Before Paul used the word (*theopneustos*) in his letter to Timothy, it seems to have appeared nowhere else in all of ancient literature. Paul points to the writings—not merely to the human authors—as communicating God's own authoritative words. When Scripture speaks, God speaks.

- God has given us his written word so that we can know the truth that saves us and leads us to righteousness (2 Timothy 3:15–17).

- In light of the Bible's divine origin, authority, and sufficiency in leading to salvation, we are called to share God's Word with others (2 Timothy 4:1–2).

Study Questions

1. Where in 2 Timothy 3:14–4:5 do you see the authority of Scripture taught?

_____

_____

_____

2. Where do you see the sufficiency of Scripture taught?

_____

_____

_____

3. Where do you see the divine origin of Scripture taught?

_____

_____

_____

4. How about Scripture's capacity to transform us?

_____

_____

_____

5. Read Romans 15:4 and 2 Peter 1:19–21. What do these verses tell us about the origin and purpose of Scripture?

_____

_____

_____

Prayer for the Road

"Father in heaven, empower us through the Holy Spirit to run the race well, keep the faith, strive toward righteousness, which is Christ Jesus, and do the good works you have prepared for us and equipped us for. In the name of Jesus, we pray. Amen." (Based on 2 Timothy 3:16–4:8).

Check This Out!

Read a brief history of the modern struggle to maintain the doctrine of inerrancy among evangelicals: "The Inerrancy of Scripture: The Fifty Years' War … and Counting" by Albert Mohler.

www.albertmohler.com/2010/08/16/the-inerrancy-of-scripture-the-fifty-years-war-and-counting

---

Review and Prepare

Day One

In *How We Got the Bible* handbook, read "Chapter 1: What's So Special about the Bible?"

What is the most important fact that you learned from this chapter?

_____

_____

_____

_____

_____

_____

Day Two

Read these statements about the Bible, spoken by early Christian leaders:

- "You have searched the Scriptures, which are true and given by the Holy Spirit. You know that nothing unrighteous or counterfeit is written in them."—Clement of Rome, 1st century

- "All Scripture, which has been given to us by God, [is] perfectly consistent. The parables harmonize with the passages that are plain; and statements with a clearer meaning serve to explain the parables." —Irenaeus of Lyons, 2nd century

- "I am entirely convinced that no Scripture contradicts another." —Justin Martyr, 2nd century

- "The statements of Holy Scripture will never contradict the truth." —Tertullian of Carthage, 3rd century

- "It is the opinion of some that the Scriptures do not agree or that the God who gave them is false. But there is no disagreement at all. Far from it! The Father, who is truth, cannot lie."—Athanasius of Alexandria, 4th century

- "I have learned to give respect and honor to the canonical books of Scripture. Regarding these books alone, I most firmly believe that their authors were completely free from error. If in these writings I am confused by anything which appears to me opposed to the truth, I do not hesitate to suppose that either the manuscript is faulty, or the translator has not caught the meaning of what was said, or I myself have failed to understand it."—Augustine of Hippo, 5th century

Summarize in one sentence how early Christians viewed the Scriptures:

_____

_____

_____

_____

_____

_____

Day Three

Read John 15:26–16:15.

Describe in your own words how the Holy Spirit illumines God's Word.

_____

_____

_____

_____

_____

_____

_____

The Holy Spirit is the Spirit of truth; any truth that comes from the Spirit originates with the Father and exalts the Son (John 15:26; 16:12–13). This same Holy Spirit inspired Scripture in the first place (2 Peter 1:21). The Holy Spirit will never illumine an application of the text of Scripture that contradicts sound interpretation of the text.

Day Four

Suppose that an unbelieving friend begins reading the Bible at the beginning. A few weeks later, the friend asks you, "Why did God give rules for how to treat slaves? And he allowed men to have multiple wives and concubines! How can your God be okay with slavery and polygamy?" How would you respond? Here are three truths that might help you:

1. **Description of an event in God's Word doesn't necessarily imply God's approval:** Some things are described in Scripture because they really happened—but that doesn't mean that God approved them. Scripture rightly records what happened even when what happened wasn't right. The Bible describes polygamy, for example, not because this practice was part of God's design for humanity but because this practice happened in the context of God's work to redeem humanity. In some cases, God provided laws to govern particular practices that were already taking place, such as slavery and divorce, to protect vulnerable populations against exploitation (see, for examples, Deuteronomy 15:12–18; 22:13–30; 24:1–4; Matthew 19:7–9; 1 Corinthians 7:20–23). Any accurate and reliable history will include descriptions of sin, since every human being other than Jesus has been a sinner. This does not mean, however, that God condoned wrongdoing. If God could condone or ignore sin, the death of Jesus on the cross would have been unnecessary.

2. **Cultural practices sometimes take different forms while maintaining the same meaning:** Some things were cultural practices, and the way these practices are expressed has changed from their culture to our culture. Have you ever wondered why we no longer greet each other with a "holy kiss"? (Romans 16:16; 1 Corinthians 16:20; 2 Corinthians 13:12; 1 Thessalonians 5:26; 1 Peter 5:14). In the early centuries of Christian worship, this became known as "the kiss of peace," which was replaced by bowing to one another and eventually—in most Western cultures—by shaking hands. Today, in Western culture, the handshake has almost entirely replaced the holy kiss as a form of Christian greeting.

Why? Because it was the principle of honoring, serving, expressing love to one another that was to be expressed and not necessarily the specific act of kissing.

3. **Some practices are fulfilled in Jesus:** Some things promised, predicted, or practiced in the Old Testament have been fulfilled in Jesus Christ. Why don't Christians sacrifice animals, for example? Because Jesus' sacrificial death on the cross has put sinful people right with God. For those who have trusted in Jesus Christ as their Savior, the sin that fractured our relationship with God has been atoned; there is no longer any need for animal sacrifices that symbolize the death of Jesus on the cross. The Old Testament laws have been fulfilled through the life, death, and resurrection of Jesus.

Write below how you would respond to your friend's questions:

_____

_____

_____

_____

_____

_____

_____

_____

_____

_____

_____

_____

Day Five

Read Nehemiah 7:73–8:18.

What does this Bible passage tell you about how the Israelites viewed the Word of God?

_____

_____

_____

_____

_____

_____

_____

_____

_____

_____

_____

_____

_____

Notes:

Notes:

SESSION 2

How We Got the Old Testament

Get This: Jesus trusted the Old Testament; so should we.

"So Ezra the priest brought the Law before the assembly, both men and women and all who could understand what they heard. … And the ears of all the people were attentive to the Book of the Law."—Nehemiah 8:2–3

Session 2 Outline

Use this session outline to follow along with the video and take notes.

1. Do we need the Old Testament?

   a. Some stories can't be started in the center.

   b. The Old Testament is the first part of the story of Jesus.

2. Who wrote the Old Testament?

   a. God etched the Ten Commandments (Exodus 32:16).

   b. Moses was the human source of the Torah (Exodus 17:14; Mark 12:26).

   c. Kings were to keep a copy of God's law (Deuteronomy 17:18–20).

   d. Ezra the scribe wrote later parts of the Old Testament.

3. How were the books of the Old Testament arranged?

   a. Torah (Law)

   b. Prophets - *Jordan judges*

c. Writings (Also called Psalms)

Potry of Daniel, - I Chut
Psalms

4. How was the Old Testament written and copied?

   a. *Old* Paleo-Hebrew, square-script Hebrew, Aramaic (Nehemiah 8:8)

      Jew Potery

   b. Masoretic scribes (5th century AD)

   c. Dead Sea Scrolls

5. Which books belong in the Old Testament?

   a. Canon — *River side Reed*
      Cut it into — Meaane —

   b. Septuagint (LXX)
      Rearranged the Book
      greek - Translation -

   c. Jerome did not consider the Apocrypha to be authoritative.
      Latin Translated -

   d. Augustine of Hippo disagreed and considered the Apocrypha to be authoritative. — *4 d 5th Century .*

   e. Jesus didn't recognize the Apocrypha as God's Word (Luke 24:44; 11:51). — *Hebrew and Cannon of Scripture*

Key Terms

Apocrypha—The name given to a collection of books that were thought to contain "hidden" or "secret" truths (from the Greek *apokrypha,* "hidden"). The books of the Apocrypha are considered canonical by the Roman Catholic and Orthodox Churches but are not included in the Jewish or most Protestant Scriptures. The Apocrypha includes books such as 1 and 2 Maccabees and Wisdom of Solomon.

Canon—(from Greek *kanon,* "measuring stick") Religious texts that are authoritative for members of that particular religion. The canon of the Bible refers to the collection of books in the Bible recognized as the authoritative Word of God.

Codex—The "book" form of ancient manuscripts, made up of a number of sheets of papyrus or parchment stacked and bound by fixing one edge (from Latin *caudex,* "block"). The codex was sometimes used by the Romans for business and legal transactions. Early Christians gathered the New Testament books in codex form.

Dead Sea Scrolls—Collection of more than 900 manuscripts (mostly in fragments) discovered by shepherds in 1947 in caves near the Dead Sea. These scrolls include portions or complete texts of all the books of the Old Testament except Esther, as well as many nonbiblical texts. The scrolls have assisted scholars in understanding the form of the text of the Hebrew and Aramaic Bible centuries before the Masoretic Text.

Jerome (c. AD 345–420)—Prolific scholar of the early church. His greatest achievement was translating Scripture from the original languages into Latin (called the Vulgate). He advocated the acceptance of the Hebrew and Aramaic canon of Scripture by the Church, thereby excluding the books that came to be called "Apocrypha."

Ketuvim (Writings)—The third section of the Hebrew canon, the Writings (sometimes known by its Latin name, *hagiographa*). The books in this section are Psalms, Job, Proverbs, Ruth, Song of Solomon (Song of Songs), Ecclesiastes, Lamentations, Esther, Daniel, Ezra, Nehemiah and 1 and 2 Chronicles.

Masoretes—Copyists who preserved the traditional text of the Hebrew beginning as early as the 5th or 6th century AD. The most famous Masoretes were the Ben Asher family who copied the oldest surviving Old Testament codexes. The text preserved by the Masoretes is known as the Masoretic Text.

Neviim (Prophets)—The second part of the Hebrew canon, including the Former and Latter Prophets. The Former Prophets include Joshua, Judges, 1 and 2 Samuel, 1 and 2 Kings. The Latter Prophets are Isaiah, Jeremiah, Ezekiel and the Twelve (Hosea, Joel, Amos, Obadiah, Jonah, Micah, Nahum, Habakkuk, Zephaniah, Haggai, Zechariah, Malachi).

Old Testament—The first part of the Christian Bible, which tells the story of God's work with the descendants of Abraham and points forward to the New Testament fulfillment of this story in Jesus. The Old Testament was written primarily in Hebrew, with a few portions preserved in a related language known as Aramaic. "Testament" translates a Greek word that could also be rendered "covenant" (2 Corinthians 3:14; Hebrews 8:13). Also known as the Hebrew Scriptures, the Jewish Scriptures, or the First Testament.

Septuagint—Greek translation of the Hebrew Bible. This Greek translation was undertaken by the Greek-speaking Jews in Alexandria from the 3rd to the 2nd century BC. Later legend claimed that seventy-two Jewish scholars completed the translation in seventy-two days, working separately by invitation from Ptolemy II Philadelphus (285–246 BC). *Septuagint* comes from the Latin term for "seventy," and the abbreviation LXX is the Roman numeral for seventy.

Tanak (also TNK, Tanakh)—Acronym for the Hebrew Scriptures: Torah (Law), Neviim (Prophets), Ketuvim (Writings).

Torah (Law)—The first part of the Hebrew canon, also known as the Pentateuch. The books in the Torah are Genesis, Exodus, Leviticus, Numbers, and Deuteronomy. Torah is sometimes translated "law." "The Law and the Prophets" could occasionally be used to refer to the Old Testament as a whole.

Group Discussion

1. If you stopped studying the Old Testament, how would that change your prayer, worship, and how you think about God?

   _____

   _____

   _____

2. Read Isaiah 40:8, Matthew 5:18, and Mark 13:31. Do these passages give you confidence that God has preserved his Word throughout time? How can this confidence change the way you read your Bible?

   _____

   _____

   _____

3. Another name for the Old Testament is the "old covenant." Covenants in the Bible are agreements and promises between two parties. The Old Testament tells the story of God's covenants with Israel and its authors looked forward to the "new covenant" or "new testament" that would be fulfilled in Jesus Christ (Jeremiah 31:31–32; Luke 22:20; 1 Corinthians 11:25; 2 Corinthians 3:6; Hebrews 8:1–13; 9:15; 12:24). When you consider how God has kept his promises—his covenants—how is your trust in him and the reliability of his Word affected?

   _____

   _____

   _____

   How would strengthened trust in God and his promises help you in your life right now?

   _____

   _____

   _____

Hear God's Word

Nehemiah 7:73–8:18

Study Notes

- The "people" are the key characters in this passage as the word occurs sixteen times in 7:73–8:18. In eleven of those occurrences, "all the people" are mentioned. It seems that Ezra's role in this passage is reading the book, but the focus is on the people and their reaction to hearing the reading of the Law. The emphasis in this passage is on the people's response to hearing God's word. Their attentiveness (8:3), posture of respect (8:5), worship (8:6), posture of submission (8:6), and their repentance (8:9) display the proper reaction of the believer upon encountering God through the Scriptures. One commentator reminds us:

  > "The Word of God, when read, has the power to transform lives today just as it had in the time of both Josiah and Ezra. The Bible convicts, changes, and guides lives. In the time of Ezra the people realized that the Babylonian captivity was a result of disobedience. Only genuine repentance before God could bring about a real change in the community. The living power of the Word of God still liberates people from their own various forms of captivity. Leaders pointed out God's mercy to the people. Those who teach must show God's justice and the need for repentance but must not forget to emphasize God's love and mercy." (Mervin Breneman, *Ezra, Nehemiah, Esther* [Nashville: Broadman & Holman Publishers, 1993], 227.)

- Sin is any offense or rebellion against God. When we are confronted with our own offenses, we are filled with sorrow in the face of God's holiness and goodness. In 8:9–12, the people experienced these exact feelings, but Nehemiah and Ezra implored them to rejoice and celebrate because (1) they had heard and responded to God's Word, and (2) this was a day to celebrate God's deliverance (Leviticus 23:23–25; Deuteronomy 16:15).

Study Questions

1. What does Nehemiah 8 tell us about the reverence and seriousness of the people as they received the Word of God?

2. Who is included in the assembly of people throughout 7:73–8:18?

3. Throughout the passage, we see the different reactions and emotions of mourning, sorrow, and rejoicing. What were the different reasons for this?

Prayer for the Road

"Father in heaven, may your Word never depart from our hearts and lips. If we ever find ourselves wandering in the wilderness of disobedience, bring us back quickly Lord to repentance and rejoicing at the sound of your voice through your written Word."

Check This Out!

View the Dead Sea Scrolls online at The Digital Dead Sea Scrolls.

http://dss.collections.imj.org.il

Review and Prepare

Day One

In *How We Got the Bible* handbook, read "How We Got the Old Testament" and "Chapter 2: How Did the Old Testament Get from God to You?"

Meditate on Isaiah 40:6–8.

How has your study of *How We Got the Bible* given more meaning to these words from the prophet Isaiah?

_____

_____

_____

_____

_____

_____

Day Two

In *How We Got the Bible* handbook, read "Chapter 3: Which Books Belong in the Old Testament?"

Meditate on Luke 24:36–49.

How did reading chapter 3 in the handbook help you to understand better what Jesus meant when he mentioned "the Law, the Prophets, and the Psalms"?

_____

_____

_____

_____

_____

_____

Day Three

Read Matthew 5:17–20 and 22:29–33.

What do these verses teach you about how Jesus viewed the Old Testament?

Jesus criticized the religious leaders' misuse of his Father's words—but he never corrected or contradicted the Old Testament laws and prophecies. Instead, he fulfilled them, and he treated them as the unerring revelation of his Father's will. The earliest Christians revered the Old Testament as God's Word because their Savior had recognized the Old Testament as God's Word.

Day Four

Study Luke 1:1–4; John 19:35; 21:24; 2 Peter 1:16–21.

Based on these texts, what value did early Christians place on eyewitness testimony about Jesus?

Day Five

Study 1 Corinthians 15:1–11.

What does this Bible passage tell you about the importance of eyewitness testimony to the resurrection among early Christians?

Notes:

Notes:

How We Got the New Testament

Get This: The testimony in the New Testament is trustworthy.

"For I delivered to you as of first importance what I also received: that Christ died for our sins in accordance with the Scriptures, that he was buried, that he was raised on the third day in accordance with the Scriptures, and that he appeared to Cephas, then to the twelve. Then he appeared to more than five hundred brothers at one time, most of whom are still alive, though some have fallen asleep."—1 Corinthians 15:3–6

Session 3 Outline

Use this session outline to follow along with the video and take notes.

1. When was the New Testament written?

   a. Paul's letter to the Galatians (AD 49)

   b. 1 and 2 Thessalonians (early AD 50s)

2. Oral histories of Jesus

   a. Stories were shared in a culture of memorization.

   b. Believers cared deeply about preserving the message of eyewitnesses.

      i. Luke (Luke 1:2)

      ii. Papias (1st century AD)

      iii. Pastor disciplined for fabricating stories about Paul in "Acts of Paul" (AD 160)

    c. Oral histories were written down before eyewitnesses passed away (1 Corinthians 15:3–8).

3.   Why did Christians write the New Testament texts?

    a. Letters to address specific issues in churches

    b. Loss of eyewitnesses

4.   The four Gospels

    a. Mark was the apostle Peter's translator.

    b. Matthew likely wrote in Aramaic; translated into Greek.

    c. Luke investigated and got stories from eyewitnesses.

    d. John was an eyewitness.

Key Terms

Autographs—The original manuscripts of the Bible in their final form are known as the *autographs*. The autographs of the New Testament decayed into dust centuries ago—but there is some evidence that the autographs might have survived at least until the end of the second century.

Gospel—(from Old English *godspel,* translation of Greek *euangelion,* "good news")

(1) gospel: Outside the New Testament in the first century AD, the word translated "gospel" referred to the proclamation of an event—such as a victory in battle or the rise of a new king—that changed the hearer's status and called for a response. In the New Testament, "gospel" came to mean the proclamation that the power of God's kingdom had entered human history through Jesus Christ to renew the whole world by means of his perfect life, substitutionary death, and victorious resurrection. When we trust what Jesus did—instead of what we can do—to be made right with God, God restores us to union with himself and communion with others.

(2) Gospel: A text that narrates the life, death, and resurrection of Jesus Christ. The four New Testament Gospels—Matthew, Mark, Luke, and John—are ancient biographies (Greek, *bioi*) and were clearly intended to be read as historical testimonies.

New Testament—The second part of the Christian Bible, which announces the fulfillment of God's Old Testament promises and the arrival of God's kingdom on earth through the perfect life, sacrificial death, and triumphant resurrection of Jesus Christ. The New Testament was originally written in Greek. "Testament" translates a Greek word that can also be rendered "covenant" (Luke 22:20; Hebrews 8:8–13).

Oral Culture—A culture in which stories and memories are recalled and shared primarily through spoken words instead of written words. In the oral culture of the first Christians, rhythmic patterns and mnemonic devices were woven into oral histories so that learners could quickly convert spoken testimonies into permanent memories. God worked through this cultural pattern to preserve the truths that we read today in the New Testament.

Oral Histories—Spoken testimonies which were memorized and shared in communities during the lifetimes of the eyewitnesses.

Group Discussion

1. Compared to other ancient historical writings, the New Testament books were written not long after the events they describe—during the lifetime of eyewitnesses, in fact! Why do you think these eyewitness accounts are criticized and mistrusted by secular historians, even though other ancient eyewitness testimonies are accepted without question?

2. The Gospel is historically trustworthy. How does this truth impact your everyday life?

3. Early Christians cared deeply about preserving and passing on the message of the eyewitnesses. Does your own life reflect that same passion? What are some things you can do to help more people hear or read this message?

Hear God's Word

1 Corinthians 15:1–11

Study Notes

- Sixteenth-century church reformer Martin Luther claimed that if anyone rejects the resurrection of Jesus, "he must deny in a lump the Gospel and everything that is proclaimed of Christ and of God. For all of this is linked together like a chain. . . . Whoever denies this article must simultaneously deny far more . . . that God is God." (Commentary on 1 Corinthians)

- The phrase, "resurrection of the dead" (one might also translate this phrase as "the standing of dead ones") meant just that! The notion of a spiritual (non-physical) resurrection—an idea that appeals to so many today—would have been incomprehensible to first-century Jews.

- Notice that Paul does not argue for the reality of Jesus' resurrection here; he assumes it for the purpose of a larger argument. How did Paul know the event was indeed real? It was part of the eyewitness testimony he received after (or at the time of) his conversion (15:3). "Paul establishes that it was something he received and passed on to them like a baton. He stresses the continuity of tradition. 'Among the first things' means 'the most important things,' or 'things of first importance.' What was first in importance was also probably spoken first." (David E. Garland, 1 Corinthians, *Baker Exegetical Commentary on the New Testament* [Grand Rapids, MI: Baker Academic, 2003], 683.)

- To drive home the point about the reliability of Paul's claim, see 1 Corinthians 15:5–8, where he points any potential resurrection doubters in the direction of countless eye witnesses who were still alive. The central claim of the New Testament is that Jesus was physically resurrected after being crucified. If this claim grew from decades of embellishment instead of historical truth, Jesus is dead, the apostles were liars, and our faith is vain (1 Corinthians 15:14–17). But evidences from the first and second centuries AD reveal that eyewitness testimony about Jesus emerged rapidly and circulated reliably. The New Testament texts relied on testimonies from apostolic eyewitnesses, and all of these texts were completed while the eyewitnesses were still alive.

Study Questions

1. What are the essential truths of the gospel message as told by Paul in 1 Corinthians 15:1–11?

2. What assurances does Paul give the church in Corinth on the basis of the resurrection of Jesus?

3. In your own words, what is Paul's main point that he wants to emphasize to the believers in Corinth in verse 11?

Prayer for the Road

"Father in heaven, thank you for sending your Son, the Word in flesh, and giving us Scripture, your Word written down. Help its truthfulness impact every aspect of our lives. Amen."

Check This Out!

"Beyond the Bible, what historical proofs do we have about the life of Jesus?" by Timothy Paul Jones
www.godtube.comwatch/?v=0JE2EFNU

"What are the Gnostic Gospels?" by Timothy Paul Jones
www.godtube.com/watch/?v=WDGPG7NX

Review and Prepare

Day One

In *How We Got the Bible* handbook, read "How We Got the New Testament" and "Chapter 4: Can We Trust the New Testament?"

Meditate on John 20:26–31 and 21:24–25.

How do these verses in John express the importance of eyewitness testimony among first-century Christians?

_____

_____

_____

_____

_____

_____

_____

Day Two

Read 1 Corinthians 11:23–26 and 15:1–7.

What do the words "received from" and "delivered" in this letter from the apostle Paul suggest?

_____

_____

_____

_____

_____

_____

Day Three

Based on what you've learned in this study, what would you say to a close friend if she or he came to the conclusion that the New Testament Gospels are not fact but fiction?

_____

_____

_____

_____

_____

_____

_____

_____

_____

_____

Evidence from the first century AD shows that testimonies about Jesus remained remarkably stable as they spread across the Roman Empire. Yes, two decades stood between Jesus' death and the earliest surviving records about him—but that doesn't mean that testimonies about Jesus were somehow mangled beyond recovery. There is clear evidence in Paul's letters that the New Testament authors repeated and wrote the same testimonies they received. When they composed letters and Gospels, these authors drew from oral testimonies and teachings of eyewitnesses. Sometimes, they recited exact testimonies that their readers already knew (1 Corinthians 11:23–25; 15:3–7). Other times, they applied Jesus' teachings without quoting them word for word (Romans 14:14; 1 Corinthians 7:10–11; 9:14)—but there's no evidence that the authors of the New Testament fabricated the words and works of Jesus

Day Four

Study 2 Peter 1:1–2, 16–21.

Why do you think that ancient Christians chose to receive Peter's letter as Scripture?

_____

_____

_____

_____

_____

_____

_____

Day Five

Study 2 Peter 3:14–18.

Describe how Peter viewed the writings of Paul.

_____

_____

_____

_____

_____

_____

_____

Notes:

How the Books of the New Testament Were Chosen

Get This: God created the New Testament canon by inspiring the written words of Christ-commissioned eyewitnesses and their close associates.

"And count the patience of our Lord as salvation, just as our beloved brother Paul also wrote to you according to the wisdom given him, as he does in all his letters when he speaks in them of these matters. There are some things in them that are hard to understand, which the ignorant and unstable twist to their own destruction, as they do the other Scriptures."—2 Peter 3:15–16

49

Session 4 Outline

Use this session outline to follow along with the video and take notes.

1. Who created the canon of the New Testament?

   a. The canon wasn't created by any human being.

   b. Early Christians recognized a canon that God had already created.

2. First-century Christians received the writings of Christ-commissioned apostles and their close associates as authoritative.

   a. Paul: Galatians 1:1; 1 Corinthians 14:37–38

   b. Peter: 2 Peter 3:15–16

   c. Gospel writers: Luke 1:1–2; John 21:24

   d. The Muratorian Fragment: "The Shepherd" was rejected as authoritative because it was written long after the time of the apostles.

3. Did all Christians recognize the same books?

   a. 20 books of the New Testament were always recognized; 7 books questioned.

   b. "Gospel of Peter" was rejected because it was not written by Peter.

4. Some New Testament books were questioned, but later it became clear that they could be traced to Christ-commissioned eyewitnesses and their close associates.

   a. Hebrews (See Hebrews 13:23)

   b. James and Jude were half-brothers of Jesus who saw the resurrected Christ.

   c. 1 and 2 Peter, 2 and 3 John were written by eyewitnesses of Jesus.

Key Terms

Apostle—From Greek *apostolos*, "sent out," "commissioned"; a witness of the resurrection of Jesus Christ (Acts 1:22) and recipient of his teachings (Ephesians 3:5), commissioned to safeguard the gospel and to apply the teachings of Jesus in the churches. Occasionally applied more broadly to individuals sent on a mission (Acts 14:4, 14).

Athanasius (c. 296–373)—A bishop in Alexandria who championed the doctrine of the Trinity against the heretic Arius. He wrote an Easter letter in the year AD 367 which listed the same 27 books that appear in the New Testament today.

Irenaeus (c. 130–c. 200)—As a pastor seeking to care for his people, Irenaeus came into sharp dispute with certain Gnostics who denied Christ's humanity. Around AD 180, Irenaeus wrote *Against Heresies* in which he mentioned all four Gospels in order along with their origins.

Lost Gospels—The term "lost Gospels" usually refers to ancient writings that were excluded from the New Testament, even though they included supposed recollections of events and teachings from the life of Jesus. Complete manuscripts of a few of these lost Gospels have survived. Others survive only in tiny fragments of papyrus or in brief quotations found in the writings of early Christian scholars. Several lost Gospels were discovered anew in the past 100 years. Copies of some texts—such as *Gospel of Philip, Gospel of Thomas, Gospel of Truth,* and *Coptic Gospel of the Egyptians*—were unearthed in 1945 in Egypt, near a village known as Nag Hammadi. If a Gospel is defined as an ancient retelling of the events or teachings from Jesus' life, there are fewer than 30 known Gospels. Unlike the New Testament Gospels, many lost Gospels record only isolated teachings or fragmentary incidents from the life of Jesus.

Muratorian Fragment—First known listing of Christian writings that were received as authoritative and publicly read in the churches; so called because it's recorded on a fragment discovered by a man named Ludovico Muratori around 1740. No one knows who recorded this list; the list seems to have been written in the vicinity of Rome in the second half of the second century and may have originated in a gathering of church leaders. The list includes all the books that appear in the New Testament today except Hebrews, James, 1 and 2 Peter, and 2 and 3 John.

Group Discussion

1. Why is it important to say that early Christians *recognized* the canon of Scripture instead of *created* it? What beliefs about God and his Word are we communicating by saying "recognized" instead of "created"?

2. Many writings that early Christians considered helpful and beneficial *are not* a part of the canon. What does this suggest about the New Testament books that *are* in the Bible?

3. Except for a few texts on the fringes of the canon, Christians throughout the world recognized the books of the New Testament as Scripture from the time they were written. How does this show God's faithfulness in giving us his Word? How should this affect our attitude toward the Bible and its impact in our lives?

Hear God's Word

2 Peter 1:1–2; 3:14–18

Study Notes

- Peter was one of the twelve original apostles and was an eyewitness to everything Scripture tells us about Jesus' ministry, death, resurrection, and ascension. Not only was he an apostle, but he was also one of Christ's closest friends and a leader of the early church after Jesus returned to the Father.

- "Faith" (2 Peter 1:1) can refer to trust in and commitment to Jesus Christ, or to a body of authoritative teaching, or else, to the Christian faith as a religious movement. In light of this translation issue, we could translate "To those who have obtained a faith" as "To you who have received the true doctrine about Jesus Christ," or "To you who God has caused to trust in Jesus Christ." (Arichea and Hatton, *A Handbook on the Letter*, 66.)

- "Our beloved brother" (3:15): Paul was Peter's "beloved brother," that is, a coworker in the gospel and fellow believer. Paul is also "our" brother, suggesting that Paul was a fellow worker and fellow apostle with Peter. Paul himself often emphasized that his apostolic calling was given by God (Romans 12:3; 15:15; 1 Corinthians 3:10; Galatians 2:9; Ephesians 3:2, 7; Colossians 1:25); Peter clearly agreed.

- "According to the wisdom given him" (3:15): God was the source of Paul's wisdom.

- "Ignorant" (3:16) translates a word used nowhere else in the New Testament. It means not simply ignorant but "unlearned," "uneducated," "uninstructed," and is used primarily of people who have not received sufficient instruction in the interpretation of Scripture and are therefore prone to error. "Unstable" on the other hand describes those who are not firmly rooted in the teachings of the Christian faith and are therefore easily misled. The same word is used in 2:14, where it is translated as "unsteady."

Study Questions

1. What reasons did Peter give his readers to pay attention to this writing?

2. What do these words from Peter imply about Paul?

3. How does Peter describe the error of false teachers? How does Peter encourage his readers to combat these teachings?

Prayer for the Road

"Father in heaven, by your grace, help us to grow in our understanding of your Word. In this journey, protect us from error in our own thoughts and the false teaching of others. Amen."

Check This Out!

"How was it decided which books would be put in the Bible?" by Timothy Paul Jones
www.godtube.com/watch/?v=0J0C01NU

Articles about the development of the New Testament canon
http://michaeljkruger.com/articles

Review and Prepare

Day One

In *How We Got the Bible* handbook, read "Chapter 5: Who Created the New Testament Canon?"

Meditate on 2 Peter 3:14–18.

How has this study helped you to see the importance of Peter's recognition of the writings of Paul as Scripture?

Day Two

Read each of the Bible passages listed in this table. Carefully consider how each New Testament book is connected to an eyewitness or a close associate of an eyewitness of the risen Lord Jesus.

Book	Author
Matthew	Matthew, apostle and eyewitness of the risen Lord (Matthew 9:9; 10:3; Acts 1:13)
Mark	Mark, traveling companion and translator for Simon Peter (1 Peter 1:13); "Mark, in his capacity as Peter's interpreter, wrote down accurately as much as he remembered." (Papias of Hierapolis, 2nd century)
Luke and Acts	Luke, traveling companion with Paul (Colossians 4:14; 2 Timothy 4:11); "Luke—the attendant of Paul—recorded in a book the Gospel that Paul declared." (Irenaeus of Lyon, 2nd century)
John	John, apostle and eyewitness of the risen Lord (Matthew 4:21; 10:2; Acts 1:13)
Romans, 1 and 2 Corinthians, Galatians, Ephesians, Philippians, Colossians, 1 and 2 Thessalonians, 1 and 2 Timothy, Titus, Philemon	Paul, apostle and later eyewitness of the risen Lord (1 Corinthians 9:1; 15:8–10). Some scholars deny that Paul authored some of these texts because of changes in the writing style; however, since Paul wrote these letters over a period of two decades and composed them with a secretary, a change in style does not necessarily indicate a change in authorship.
Hebrews	Received by early Christians as a proclamation from Paul or as a reliable reflection of Paul's theology written by someone else, based on the mention of Timothy (Hebrews 13:23). "Who wrote it, in truth, God only knows." (Origen of Alexandria, 3rd century)

Book	Author
James	James the Just, relative of Jesus and eyewitness of the risen Lord, recognized later as an apostle (Matthew 13:55; 1 Corinthians 15:7; Galatians 1:19; 2:9)
1 and 2 Peter	Peter, apostle and eyewitness of the risen Lord (Matthew 4:18; 10:2; Acts 1:13). Second Peter is so different from 1 Peter that many scholars deny that Simon Peter wrote 2 Peter. It is more likely that the shift between the two letters is due to different circumstances and different secretaries being involved in the composition of each letter.
1 John	John, apostle and eyewitness of the risen Lord (Matthew 4:21; 10:2; Acts 1:13)
2 and 3 John	John, apostle and eyewitness of the risen Lord (Matthew 4:21; 10:2; Acts 1:13); these epistles may have been written by another eyewitness named John, known as "John the elder," mentioned by Papias of Hierapolis (2nd century).
Jude	Jude, relative of Jesus and eyewitness of the risen Lord (Matthew 13:55)
Revelation	John, apostle and eyewitness of the risen Lord (Matthew 4:21; 10:2; Acts 1:13); it is possible, though unlikely, that Revelation was written by another eyewitness named John, known as "John the elder," mentioned by Papias of Hierapolis (2nd century).

Day Three

Suppose that a friend said to you, "I learned in a documentary that the person who chose the books in the Bible was Emperor Constantine. And he made his choices 300 years after the time of Jesus! How can you believe the Bible is true if the books weren't even chosen until the fourth century?" What would you say?

_____

_____

_____

_____

_____

_____

The canon of the New Testament took shape in three phases:

1. **The creation of the canon:** As soon as a God-inspired eyewitness or associate of an eyewitness wrote words breathed out by God in the first century AD, this text was canon, whether or not everyone recognized it yet.

2. **The functional canon:** Texts were received as canon and functioned as canon in the churches. Occasionally, Christians in certain locations may have received a text as canon that wasn't really canonical at all—but the core books of the New Testament (the Gospels, Acts, Paul's letters, at least one letter from John) seem to have been received immediately and universally; there is no hint of any time when any of these texts was ever questioned.

3. **The exclusive canon:** When Athanasius of Alexandria sent out his Easter letter in AD 367, he was recognizing a consensus that had already emerged when he wrote these words. Only 27 books could be traced back to apostolic eyewitnesses and their close associates; therefore, only these 27 books were recognized as New Testament canon. (Michael Kruger, _The Question of Canon_ [Downers Grove: IVP, 2013].)

Day Four

Describe in your own words how Christians recognized the books in the New Testament as authoritative canon.

Day Five

Read John 5:3–4 and 1 John 5:7–8 in several translations of the Bible. Pay careful attention to any footnotes.

Do any of these translations have footnotes that explain differences in the Greek manuscripts of the New Testament? How do these different translations describe the differences in the Greek manuscripts?

Notes:

SESSION 5

How the New Testament Was Copied

Get This: God has preserved his Word sufficiently for us to recover the message he intended.

"The grass withers, the flower fades, but the word of our God will stand forever."—Isaiah 40:8

Session 5 Outline

Use this session outline to follow along with the video and take notes.

1. Early Christians cared deeply about maintaining the text.

   a. Warning not to add or take away words from Scripture (Revelation 22:18–19; 1st century AD)

   b. Origen of Alexandria rebuked scribes who changed the text of Scripture (3rd century AD).

   c. *Codex Vaticanus* shows a copyist chastising an earlier copyist who changed one of the readings of Scripture (4th century AD).

   d. Earliest Copies:

      i. Papyrus 52 - John 18 (2nd century AD)

      ii. Papyrus 104 - Matthew 21 (2nd century AD)

      iii. Possible fragment of Mark's Gospel (late 1st or early 2nd century AD)

      iv. Papyrus 66 and Papyrus 45 - John and Luke (about AD 200)

2. Overwhelming majority of variations have no impact on our translations.

   a. Example of a text variation: John 3:3 *Codex Sinaiticus*

   b. Most variations are things like a Greek definite article added or dropped out, a misspelling, or different word order that do not affect translation.

3. Textual criticism can recover nearly every original word.

   a. More than 5,600 New Testament fragments and manuscripts survive today.

   b. Examples of differences: John 5:4; Acts 8:37; Mark 16:8–20; John 7:53–8:11.

   c. 97–99% of the original text can be reconstructed.

4. Variations do not affect anything we believe about God or his work.

   a. Example: John 1:18, compare with John 20:28; 3:16. Jesus is both the Son and God.

Key Terms

Codex—(from Latin *caudex*, "block") The book form of ancient manuscripts, made up of sheets of papyrus or parchment stacked and bound by fixing one edge. The codex was sometimes used by the Romans for business and legal transactions. Early Christians gathered the New Testament books in codex form.

Codex Sinaiticus—Codex Sinaiticus is a fourth-century Greek manuscript and generally considered to be one of the most important witnesses to the text because of its antiquity and clear concern for accuracy.

Codex Vaticanus—Codex Vaticanus is perhaps the oldest uncial manuscript and one of the most important witnesses to the text of the New Testament. It was probably copied no later than the middle of the fourth century.

Johannes Gutenberg (1397–1468)—Johannes Gutenberg, born in Mainz, Germany, is acknowledged as a key contributor to the invention of movable type printing. Gutenberg was seeking more rapid methods for producing books, which until then were produced slowly by copyists using quills and reeds or by printing with hand stamps and woodcuts. Gutenberg developed an oil-based ink and a typecasting machine that used a tin alloy to cast movable metal type. Using this method, a printer could make identical copies of a book quite quickly—about 300 copies per day.

Koine Greek—The common Greek language of the New Testament era, used by the authors of the New Testament.

Papyrus—A tall, aquatic reed that grows in the Nile Delta of Egypt and was made into a writing material of the same name. Papyrus was a primary writing surface throughout the Mediterranean world from the 4th century BC to the 7th century AD. The earliest surviving New Testament Greek manuscripts were written on papyrus.

Scribe—A person who copied ancient documents by hand as a profession. Scribes became less important with the invention of the printing press in the 15th century.

Textual Criticism—The scholarly discipline of establishing the text as near to the original as possible. Since we no longer have any original manuscripts, or "autographs," scholars must sort and evaluate the variant wordings of existing copies. The textual critic not only sorts through manuscripts and fragments for copyist errors but also considers early translations and lectionaries—church worship resources—to determine the original reading of each text.

Uncial—Writing script commonly used in manuscripts from the 4th until the 8th century AD. Uncial scripts are written in majuscule (all upper-case letters). Many important manuscripts of the New Testament—including Codex Sinaiticus and Codex Vaticanus—were written in uncial script.

Variant—Copying differences between manuscripts.

Group Discussion

1. What do issues of translation and textual criticism teach us about God's faithfulness in preserving his Word?

2. How does the truth of God's preservation of Scripture affect the way that you read the Bible?

3. In this session, we have seen how deeply early Christians cared for Scripture and how important it was to them to faithfully pass on these sacred writings. In what ways do you see Christians today caring deeply for God Word?

Are there areas where you see a lack of concern for God's Word?

Hear God's Word

John 1:14–18; 3:16; 20:28

Study Notes

The point of studying these three verses is to reinforce this truth: even if we don't know how to solve every textual variant perfectly, what we believe about God and his work in the world is not affected.

John 1:18 presents a textual difficulty. There are two primary possible readings:

(1) Some Greek manuscripts support the translation "the only God" or "one and only God" (or "only begotten God"). If this manuscript variant is correct, the verse states that Jesus is God.

(2) Other Greek manuscripts support the translation "the only Son" or "one and only Son" (or "only begotten Son"). If this manuscript variant is correct, the verse states that Jesus is the Son.

On a tiny percentage of variants, scholars aren't absolutely certain of the original reading. Not one of these uncertainties affects what we believe about God or his work in the world. John 1:18 is one example, where the reading "one and only Son" or "one and only God" are both present in different translations.

While both variants are possible, they both echo truths taught elsewhere in Scripture and both fit with what we are taught throughout John's Gospel!

- Thomas's confession in John 20:28 is one of the clearest affirmations in the New Testament that Jesus is fully God.

- The words of Jesus through John in John 3:16 clearly affirm that Jesus is the Son of God.

Nothing that we believe about Jesus is, therefore, changed because of the textual variant in John 1:18.

Study Questions

1. John's Gospel is a book-length demonstration that God himself has been revealed in the flesh among humankind. Look again at John 1:14–18. According to these verses, what was the purpose of Jesus' coming in the flesh?

2. According to John 1:14–18, what specific aspects of God's character are revealed through Jesus?

3. Thomas's confession in John 20:28 is a key moment in John's Gospel. What does this confession tell us about early Christian beliefs about Jesus?

Prayer for the Road

"Father in heaven, thank you for sending your Son—Jesus Christ, God in flesh—that we might believe he is the Christ and have eternal life in his name. Help us always to have confidence in your Word. Build us in faith according to your grace. Amen."

Check This Out!

View New Testament manuscripts online at The Center for the Study of New Testament Manuscripts.

www.csntm.org

Review and Prepare

Day One

In *How We Got the Bible* handbook, read "How the Bible Made It from Manuscripts to You" and "Chapter 6: How Was the New Testament Copied?"

Meditate on John 1:14–18. How has this study helped you to understand these verses better?

How has this study helped you to see the importance of Peter's recognition of the writings of Paul as Scripture?

Day Two

Suppose a coworker comments to you, "Even if the Bible started out as true, it's not reliable now. It's been changed so many times that no one is really sure what the text said in the first place." How would you respond?

The text of the New Testament has been preserved remarkably well. In every case in which there are copying variants and two or more options remain possible, every possible option simply reinforces truths that are already clearly present in the writings of that particular author and in the New Testament as a whole. There is no point at which any of the possible options would require readers to rethink an essential belief about Jesus or to doubt the historical integrity of the New Testament. Simply put, the differences are not highly significant, as some skeptics claim. The differences in manuscripts, whether accidental or intentional, in no way affect any Christian belief or practice.

Day Three

So how do New Testament scholars choose the reading of a text that most likely represents the original wording, especially when there are several possibilities? Here are basic principles that most textual critics follow:

1. Look *beyond* the manuscript at other manuscripts and consider:

   - which reading is *oldest,*

   - which reading is supported by texts that were separated by the *farthest distance,*

   - and to which *textual family* the manuscript belongs. Each textual family (Western, Alexandrian, or Byzantine, for example) represents a certain pattern of preservation and changes in the New Testament manuscripts. By comparing the families, textual critics are often able to determine *when* and *where* changes occurred.

2. Look *within* the manuscript for which reading is more probable based on:

   - what a copyist would be most likely to change,

   - which possible reading is shortest,

   - which reading might have been an attempt to harmonize one text with another, and

   - what difficult words a copyist might have replaced with simpler ones.

3. Look at other writings by the same original author to see which reading is most similar to the author's other writings.

Day Four

Meditate on Matthew 28:19–20.

Write your reflections below:

_____

_____

_____

_____

_____

_____

Day Five

Review Matthew 28:19–20.

Jesus commanded his followers to proclaim the gospel and to teach God's Word to every people-group. Different people-groups speak different languages. With that in mind, list the resources that believers in other people-groups need to be able to understand the Scriptures.

_____

_____

_____

_____

_____

_____

Notes:

Notes:

How We Got the Bible in English

Get This: Every person in every language needs a Bible that they can understand.

"Go therefore and make disciples of all nations, baptizing them in the name of the Father and of the Son and of the Holy Spirit."—Matthew 28:19–20

Session 6 Outline

1. John Wycliffe

Use this session outline to follow along with the video and take notes.

   a. He translated the Bible into English from Latin (1382).

   b. He was condemned (1415) and burned for heresy (1428) *after* he was dead.

   c. About a century after Wycliffe, Martin Luther translated the Bible into German (1534).

2. Three key events in the 1400s

   a. Gutenberg printing press made mass printing possible (1455).

   b. Fall of Constantinople caused Eastern Christians to flee West with their Greek New Testaments (1453).

   c. Renaissance of interest in ancient languages emerged in European universities.

3. Greek New Testament

   a. Erasmus published Latin and Greek side by side (1516).

   b. Robert Stephanus (Estienne) introduced verse divisions.

   c. *Textus Receptus* (Received Text): Greek New Testaments traced back to Erasmus

4. William Tyndale

   a. He translated the Bible into English from Greek and Hebrew (1525–1535).

   b. His translation influenced the Matthew's Bible (1537), the Great Bible (1539), and the Geneva Bible (1560).

5. King James Bible (1611)

   a. Puritans petitioned King James for reform, including a new English translation of the Bible.

   b. King James Version became the most popular English version.

6. Later English Translations

   a. Older manuscripts discovered (18th–19th centuries)

   b. English Revised Version (1885)/American Standard Version (1901)

   c. Over 900 English translations

Key Terms

Erasmus of Rotterdam (c. 1466–1536)—A Dutch biblical scholar, philologist, and textual critic. Erasmus is credited with editing the first published edition of the Greek New Testament in 1516, a text that was revised several times in the following years. The translators of the King James Version relied on a later edition of the Greek text of Erasmus when they translated the New Testament.

Geneva Bible (1560)—This Bible, used by William Shakespeare, was translated by Protestant refugees from England during the reign of Queen Mary I ("Bloody Mary"). Much of the translation was shaped by the Great Bible and Tyndale's New Testament.

Great Bible (1539)—Myles Coverdale based this Bible on the Matthew's Version. A copy of the Great Bible was placed in every church in England.

King James Version (1611)—A title used for the English translation of the Bible commonly known as the Authorized Version. Translated at the command of King James I of England. It was revised several times. The 1769 edition is the version used most widely today.

Matthew's Version—John Rogers brought together Tyndale's published and unpublished translations with Coverdale's translation of the Old Testament Prophets (as well as the Apocrypha). Published under the pseudonym "Thomas Matthew."

Robert Stephanus (Estienne)—Editor of the Stephanus Greek New Testaments. He divided biblical chapters into verses in one of his early Greek New Testaments.

Textus Receptus—Latin for "received text." Refers to the entire series of published Greek New Testaments that derive from Erasmus' text.

William Tyndale (c. 1494–1536)—A translator of the Bible, known as "the father of the English Bible." He sometimes used the pseudonym William Huchyns. Around 1522, he conceived the project of translating the Bible into English, but had to relocate to Germany to be free to do so. The printing of his first translation of the New Testament was interrupted by the local authorities but eventually completed later that year. On its arrival in England in 1526, it was bitterly attacked by local archbishops. Tyndale spent most of his remaining years at Antwerp, Belgium, where he frequently revised the

New Testament. His biblical translations, made direct from the Greek and Hebrew into straightforward and vigorous English, have influenced virtually every subsequent English translation. In 1535 he was arrested, imprisoned, strangled, and burnt at the stake.

John Wycliffe (c. 1330–1384)—English philosopher, theologian, and reformer. Wycliffe held that people need the Bible in their native language. It is uncertain whether Wycliffe took any direct part in the translation of the first entirely English Bible, but most scholars attribute to Wycliffe either oversight or inspiration of the project that eventually became known as the Wycliffe Bible.

Vulgate—The Latin translation of the Bible by Jerome in the 4th century AD (Latin *vulgo,* "to make common, accessible"). It is characterized by its adherence to the Hebrew text of the Old Testament rather than reliance on the Septuagint or some other translation. The Wycliffe Bible began as an almost word for word translation of the Latin Vulgate.

Group Discussion

1. If you could meet John Wycliffe or William Tyndale today, what would you say to them?

   _____

   _____

   _____

   _____

   _____

   _____

   _____

2. Do you think it is helpful to have so many different English translations today? Explain why or why not.

   _____

   _____

   _____

3. How should knowing that people died for their efforts to get the Bible translated into other languages impact your Bible study, prayer, and worship?

   _____

   _____

   _____

4. Nearly 2,000 people-groups have no Bible in their language. What should be our priority as we consider how to make disciples in these people-groups?

   _____

   _____

   _____

Hear God's Word

Matthew 28:19–20

Study Notes

- "Make disciples" is a command. Going, baptizing, and teaching are the means by which we are to obey Jesus' command.

- The Gospel According to Matthew began with the prophecy that Jesus would be called *Immanuel*, which means "God with us" (1:23). The book ends with Jesus promising that he is indeed with us until the end of the age (28:20).

Study Questions

1. How does the Great Commission (Matthew 28:19–20) connect to the history of the English Bible?

2. In particular, how does the Great Commission connect to the work of John Wycliffe and William Tyndale?

3. Why do we need the Scriptures to be able to make disciples in every nation?

Prayer for the Road

"Father in heaven, may your Word continue to spread to the ends of the earth and make disciples wherever it is read, preached, and heard. Give us hearts to be a part of this great work, Lord. Amen."

Check This Out!

Take a virtual tour of the Dunham Bible Museum.
www.hbu.edu/About-HBU/The-Campus/Facilities/Morris-Cultural-Arts-Center/Museums/Dunham-Bible-Museum/Tour-of-the-Museum.aspx

For statistics on the status of worldwide Bible translation efforts, check out Wycliffe Global Alliance.
www.wycliffe.net

Reflection and Prepare

Day One

In *How We Got the Bible* handbook, read "Chapter 7: Where Did the English Bible Come From?"

Write below the most important truths that you learned from this chapter.

_____

_____

_____

_____

_____

_____

_____

At this point, you might be wondering: Is there a best version of the English Bible? The "best version" sometimes depends on the needs of the reader.

- **Functional equivalent** translations follow the original text phrase by phrase instead of word by word. For newer Christians or persons for whom English is a second language, a functional equivalent version like the New Living Translation might be the best place to start.

- **Formal equivalent** translations strive to follow the wording of the Hebrew, Aramaic, and Greek texts as closely as possible. For mature Christians or for in-depth study, formal equivalent translations like the English Standard Version or the New American Standard Bible may be more appropriate.

- **A few translations**—like the Holman Christian Standard Bible, the NET Bible, and God's Word—try to balance functional and formal equivalence.

In truth, however, God can work through almost any translation of the Bible, as long as the translation seeks to state the meaning of the original texts in a new language instead of tweaking the meaning to fit a certain political or theological agenda.

Day Two

In *How We Got the Bible* handbook, review "Chapter 1: What Makes the Bible So Special?"

What are the most important truths that you learned from this chapter?

_____

_____

_____

_____

_____

_____

Day Three

In *How We Got the Bible* handbook, review "Chapter 2: How Did the Old Testament Get from God to You?" and "Chapter 3: Which Books Belong in the Old Testament?"

What are the most important truths that you learned from these chapters?

_____

_____

_____

_____

_____

_____

Day Four

In *How We Got the Bible* handbook, review "Chapter 4: Can We Trust the New Testament?" and "Chapter 5: Who Created the New Testament Canon?"

Write below the most important truths that you learned from these chapters.

_____

_____

_____

_____

_____

_____

_____

_____

_____

_____

_____

_____

_____

_____

_____

_____

_____

_____

_____

Day Five

In *How We Got the Bible* handbook, review "Chapter 6: How Was the New Testament Copied?"

What are the most important truths that you learned from this chapter?

_____

_____

_____

_____

_____

_____

_____

_____

_____

_____

> "Just as William Tyndale prayed, 'Lord, open the king of England's eyes,' perhaps our prayer should be today, 'Lord, open our eyes to the need around us,' to train translators and to send translators so that we provide the world with the Word of God."—Timothy Paul Jones

List three specific truths that you learned during this study that have transformed the way you view God's written Word.

1. _____

_____

_____

2. _____

_____

_____

3. _____

_____

_____

Take the quiz on the following page to see how much you've learned after this six-session study.

How We Got the Bible Quiz

1. How many books are in the Bible?

    _____

2. How many human authors wrote the books of the Bible?
    a. Fewer than 10
    b. Between 10 and 25
    c. At least 40
    d. More than 100

3. What do we call the original manuscripts of the Bible?

    _____

4. How many original manuscripts of the Bible survive today?

    _____

5. In what language(s) was the Old Testament originally written?

    _____

6. In what language was the New Testament originally written?

    _____

7. What do we call the ancient Greek translation of the Old Testament?

   _____

8. When did mass printing of Bibles begin?

   a. Before AD 300
   b. Around AD 650
   c. After AD 1400
   d. After AD 1750

9. How many ancient Greek manuscripts of the New Testament exist?

   a. Fewer than 1,000
   b. Between 1,000 and 2,500
   c. Between 2,500 and 5,000
   d. More than 5,000

10. Who is known as the "father of the English Bible"?

    _____

(Answers on the next page)

Answer Key

(1) 66

(2) c. At least 40

(3) Autographs

(4) Zero. There are no surviving *original* manuscripts.

(5) Hebrew (and Aramaic)

(6) Greek (or Koine Greek)

(7) Septuagint (or LXX)

(8) c. After AD 1400 (Gutenberg Printing Press about AD 1450)

(9) d. More than 5,000

(10) William Tyndale (John Wycliffe could also be a correct response.)

Notes:

Notes:

HOW WE GOT THE BIBLE

DVD Bible Study for Individual or Group Use

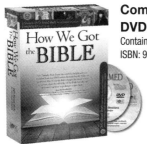

Complete *How We Got the Bible* DVD Bible Study Kit

Contains one each of the following items
ISBN: 9781628622072

How We Got the Bible DVD

• All six DVD sessions • Leader Guide on disc as a printable PDF •
Fliers, bulletin inserts, posters & banners as PDFs on disc
ISBN: 9781628622065

Leader Guide

• Leader Guide gives step-by-step instructions for group hosts or facilitators so you don't have to be the expert.
ISBN: 9781628622089

Participant Guide

• Purchase one for each participant.
• Includes group discussion questions, session outlines, key terms and definitions, Bible study questions, and more.
ISBN: 9781628622126

PowerPoint® presentation

• Contains more than 100 slides to expand the scope of the teaching ISBN: 9781890947460

Pamphlet

• Fold-out time line of key events
ISBN: 9781628620825

How We Got the Bible handbook

• Goes into more depth
• Explores the historical background
• 180-page paperback
ISBN: 9781628622164

www.hendricksonrose.com

95

FEASTS OF THE BIBLE

DVD Bible Study for Individual or Group Use

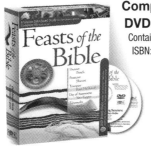

**Complete *Feasts of the Bible*
DVD Bible Study Kit**
Contains one each of everything below
ISBN: 9781596364646

Feasts of the Bible DVD
- All six DVD-based sessions
- Leader Guide on disc as a printable PDF • Fliers, bulletin inserts, posters & banners as PDFs on disc
ISBN: 9781596364653

Leader Guide
- Leader Guide gives step-by-step instructions for group hosts or facilitators so you don't have to be the expert
ISBN: 9781596364660

Participant Guide
- Each participant will need a guide
- Guide contains definitions, charts, comparisons, Bible references, discussion questions, and more
ISBN: 9781596364677

Feasts of the Bible PowerPoint® presentation
- Contains more than 100 slides to expand the scope of the teaching   ISBN: 9781596361775

Feasts of the Bible pamphlet
- Chart showing each feast, the date, biblical passage, and symbolism fulfilled by Jesus
ISBN: 9781890947583

Messiah in the Feasts of Israel handbook
- Goes into greater depth on all the feasts
- Gives insights into God's redemptive plan, discusses the prophetic purposes of the feasts
- 236-page paperback
ISBN: 9780970261977

www.hendricksonrose.com